Your Word Is Fire

THE HASIDIC MASTERS ON CONTEMPLATIVE PRAYER

Revised and Expanded Edition

Edited and Translated by
Arthur Green and **Barry W. Holtz**
with **Ariel Evan Mayse**

For People of All Faiths, All Backgrounds

JEWISH LIGHTS Publishing
Nashville, Tennessee

Jewish Lights Publishing
an imprint of Turner Publishing Company
Nashville, Tennessee
New York, New York
www.jewishlights.com
www.turnerpublishing.com

Your Word Is Fire: The Hasidic Masters on Contemplative Prayer

2nd Edition

Library of Congress Cataloging-in-Publication Data
is available from the Library of Congress

Cover design: Tim Holtz
Interior design: Tim Holtz
Printed in the United States of America
17 18 19 20 10 9 8 7 6 5 4 3 2 1

CONTENTS

TO THE READER

We are grateful that this collection of Hasidic prayer instructions has now been in print for forty years. It was originally published by the Paulist Press in an era when there was no Jewish publisher interested in such materials. It was then picked up first by Schocken Books and then by Jewish Lights. We are most grateful to Stuart Matlins, founder and longtime owner of Jewish Lights, for encouraging us to prepare this expanded edition of the work. A number of newly translated sources are included here, along with a revised introduction and a list of suggestions for further reading. When this book was first published, there were almost no resources on Jewish devotional teachings available in English. Now, thanks in large part to Jewish Lights, there is much that we can recommend.

We are most grateful to Rabbi Ariel Evan Mayse for significant contributions to this new edition, including the suggestion of new texts, translations, formatting, and editing.

INTRODUCTION

I

The world, we are told by the ancient rabbis, stands upon three pillars: study of Torah, worship, and deeds of compassion. The nature and relative importance of these three pillars of religious life—the intellectual, the devotional, and the activist—have been debated by rabbis and their disciples over the course of many centuries. It was always assumed that the three were deeply intertwined and that a proper balance among them formed the ideal of Jewish religiosity. No one of these three values was ever allowed to totally supplant the others; nevertheless, there were times and places in the history of Judaism in which one pillar or another seemed to achieve primacy in the minds of pious reflecting Jews.

This is nowhere as clear as in the early period of Hasidism, the great movement of religious revival that brought new spirit to the lives of Jews in the towns and villages of Poland and the Ukraine toward the latter half of the eighteenth century. Here worship, particularly in the form of contemplative prayer, came to be clearly identified by a new group of religious teachers as the central focus of the Jew's religious life. Both the ecstatic outpourings of ordinary people and the highly sophisticated treatments of devotional psychology in the works of early Hasidic masters bear witness to this new and unique emphasis upon the inner life of prayer.

Surely one of the most controversial and often misunderstood movements in Jewish history, Hasidism has undergone several major transformations in the course of its nearly two and a half centuries. Originally seeing itself as a movement of renewal within a wholly traditional, if often spiritually dulled, Jewish community, Hasidism later took on the task of defending tradition and offering a bastion of resistance to Jews who sought to reject the values of modernity. From that point, early in the nineteenth century, it came to be increasingly identified with the old Jewish way of life, opposed to all change. In our day Hasidism is known as a form of Jewish ultra-Orthodoxy.

But this was hardly the case in the movement's early days. Then the newly emerging circles of teachers and disciples were seen as often unwelcome "newcomers" in the established communities. The values they taught often seemed at odds with the great Jewish traditions of learning and threatening to those who embodied them. Three times, in the course of Hasidism's early spread, rabbis and communal authorities joined in an attempt to destroy the new movement by excommunicating its leaders and those who followed their ways.

What was it that these new masters taught? Their message was simple and in itself wholly traditional, but its challenge to established religion and religious authorities was hardly hidden from view. The early Hasidic masters saw all of Jewish life as "the way of service." Our only task in this world, they taught, is the service of God. Prayer, study, and all of the commandments are to be seen instrumentally: they are the means by which the Jew may fulfill this sacred task. Thus the rabbinic ideal of "study for its own sake" had to be scrutinized and reinterpreted as study for the sake of God, a conscious act of worship. Hasidic authors tirelessly warned their readers against the dangers of robot-like performance of the commandments. Each ritual act must have its way lighted by the glow of inner devotion, else it "has no wings" and cannot ascend to God. Even acts of human kindness, the "deeds of compassion" of which the rabbis had spoken, were seen in devotional terms: there is no higher sacred act than that of helping another to discover the presence of God within his or her own soul.

The core of "service" as seen in early Hasidism is the fulfillment of that desire, deeply implanted within each human soul, to return to its original state, to be one with God. Prayer, by its very nature pointing to the intimate relationship between God and soul, becomes the focal point of Hasidic religiosity. The Ba'al Shem Tov

(1700–1760), the first great master of the movement, was told by heaven that all his spiritual attainments derived not from any claim to scholarship (as was commonly to be expected in non-Hasidic circles of the time), but rather from the great devotion with which he prayed.

The ecstatic quality of prayer life in early Hasidism has been described in many ways. The Ba'al Shem Tov was said to tremble so greatly in his prayer that bits of grain in a nearby barrel were seen to join him in his trembling. A disciple who touched the master's prayer-garment was so seized with tremors that he had to pray for release. One of the followers was so overcome by ecstasy while preparing for prayer in the ritual bath that he ran from the bathhouse to the adjoining synagogue and danced on the tables without realizing he was not fully dressed. Strange and seemingly inhuman noises, violent movements of the body, even the turning of cartwheels before the Torah, all characterized the devotional climate of some early Hasidic groups. The masters themselves sometimes felt called upon to restore the values of inwardness and silence to a world where unbridled mystical ecstasy was coming to be the order of the day.

What was it about, all this ecstatic frenzy? Prayer was surely not a new discovery for the Jew in the eighteenth century. For nearly two thousand years pious Jews had been reciting their prescribed daily prayers, morning, afternoon, and evening. Private prayers, offered either in Hebrew or in one's spoken tongue, were always considered welcome additions to the fixed liturgy. It had been said of the second-century Rabbi Akiva that if you left him praying in one corner of a room, you were sure to return to find him in the opposite corner, so enthusiastic was his style of worship. Medieval mystics in Germany, France, and Spain had devoted much of their attention to the secrets of inward prayer, turning the recitation of the obligatory liturgy into a setting for the ascent of the soul into ever-higher realms of spiritual existence. Why then all the commotion about prayer at this late date, to the point that the great rabbis of the day were confused and frightened by the forms worship took in the emerging movement?

In order to understand this renewed excitement over prayer, we must realize that Hasidism was, in the truest sense, a revival movement, one that sought to bring new life to old forms that are ever faced with the dangers of petrification and decay. The strength of Judaism has always been its ability to at once preserve and renew its most ancient forms. This is also true with regard to liturgical prayer. The power of liturgy lies largely in its familiarity. The worshiper is enriched by the sense of the words' antiquity: we pray today as did our most ancient ancestors, as our descendants will down to the end of time. So it seems from within the traditional community of prayer. But in this very sameness and constant repetition lies the potential downfall of such prayer, which can degenerate into mere mechanistic recitation. The Ba'al Shem Tov and his followers were acutely aware of this problem. They knew that prayer could only work if it were a constant source for the rediscovery of God's presence throughout the world.

The mystical ecstasy of Hasidism flows from the rediscovery that God is present in all of human life. All things and all moments are vessels that contain the Presence. The prophet's cry "The whole earth is filled with His glory!" and the old Kabbalistic formula "There is no place devoid of Him" became ecstatic watchwords in early Hasidism. Since all of Creation is filled with God's Presence, there is neither place nor moment that cannot become an opening in which one may encounter God. Hasidism thus teaches that all of life is an extension of the hour of prayer and that prayer itself is the focal point around which one's entire day is centered.

The followers of the Ba'al Shem Tov were not the first to assert the primacy of prayer in Judaism. For two hundred years before the birth of Hasidism, the mystic teachers who followed in the path of Rabbi Isaac Luria (1534–1572) of Safed had already placed boundless store in the power of man to uplift the fallen world by means of meditative prayer. Lurianic prayer was filled with a kind of urgent and theurgic messianism: by means of an infinitely complex system of theosophical meditations, in which each word and letter was used to address a particular configuration of the divine potencies, prayer could help to bring about the long-awaited redemption of Israel and the world.

Hasidism continued in the Lurianic path, but with two important changes. From the outset, Hasidic piety contained within it an ideal of simplicity. Hasidism may indeed be viewed socially as both the political and spiritual self-assertion of the more modestly educated lower classes against the elitism of the abstrusely learned. Thus the complex contemplative system of the Lurianic Kabbalists, which itself required a great deal of esoteric learning, became intolerable as an ideal. The word spoken with simple wholeness of heart came to be more highly valued than that spoken with deep knowledge of esoteric symbols: the depths of contemplation became open to all who sought truly to enter them. One of the masters explained this change in values by the parable of the keys and the lock. In former times, the mystics had access to a complicated series of keys that could unlock the heart in prayer. We no longer have the keys; all we can do is to smash the lock. The only true prerequisite for such prayer, he said, is a broken heart.

The nature of the redemption to be brought about by prayer and observance of the commandments was also transformed in Hasidism. Largely because of the tragic failure of messianism in the previous century's Sabbatian uprising, the use of prayer as a direct vehicle for historic redemption was downplayed in Hasidic teachings. By means of *devekut*, or intimate attachment to God, one could come to personally transcend all the trials of life in the world, while the external historical situation in fact remained unchanged. Redemption *within* this world became the goal. For some Hasidic authors, the *devekut* state as attained by the individual came to replace *tikkun*, eschatological world-redemption, as the central goal of the religious life.

II

The revolution contained in the Hasidic attitude toward liturgical prayer was perhaps best expressed by Rabbi Pinhas of Korets. "People think," he said, "that they pray to God. But this is not the case. For prayer itself is of the essence of God!" Prayer is God! The statement seems, at first reading, to be simply an outpouring of ecstasy, the particular meaning of which is difficult to determine. But in fact such a statement is a radical formulation of deeply rooted Hasidic ideas, which form the background of the movement's fascination with prayer.

The human soul, according to Hasidic teaching, is "a part of God above." Religious devotion is caused by the longing of the soul to be reunited with its source, from which it has been separated in the process of human individuation. While souls differ from one another in their inner nature according to their various "roots" or origin above, and while each soul must find its own individual path to *devekut*, all souls can come together in the outpouring process of prayer. Prayer, and particularly the traditional Hebrew prayers of the liturgy, is the vehicle through which the spark of God within the soul may come face-to-face with the God beyond. Thus prayer itself is the process of *yihud*, the unification of God, always proclaimed by the Kabbalists to be the highest goal of life.

This glorification of the text of prayer is further rooted in the fascination with the mystery of the word, which has always characterized Jewish spirituality. The biblical account of Creation, in which God creates the world by the mysterious power of speech, plays a formative role in all of later Jewish piety. Augmented by the Kabbalistic Creation myth, in which God is said to create through permutations of chains of Hebrew letters, it sets the mysticism of words and letters as one of the central themes of Jewish religious literature. Liturgical prayer recited in the holy tongue, says the Hasidic masters, is but a reordering of the letters, forms them into words of prayer, and brings them back to God. Thus soul and word are undergoing the same process in prayer: they help to carry one another in their shared journey of return to their source in God. In order to pray deeply, a person must truly enter into the letters, until the light of God's Creation, which still dwells within them, is seen.

The centrality of word and letter mysticism in Hasidic thinking is perhaps best illustrated by a well-known story, various versions of which are often quoted in the name of the Hasidic masters. There was once a simple man who used to address God in prayer by saying,

"Lord of the World! You know that I have not studied, that I cannot even read the holy words of Your prayer book. All I remember of that which I learned as child is the alphabet itself. But surely You, Lord, know all the words. So I will give you the letters of the alphabet, and You can form the words Yourself." And so he prayed, reciting the letters of the alphabet: "*Aleph, bet, gimel ...*"

The story, like many Hasidic tales, is not so simple as it first appears. Here two of the great ideals of Hasidic devotion have been combined: the virtue of simplicity and the fascination with the creative powers of the letters, the building blocks of both divine and human speech. The divine energy of Creation formed the universe through the powers of the word; God's speech, in fact, like human speech, may be made accessible if reduced to the constituent letters of the alphabet. In the tale, the simple man has nothing to offer to God but the letters. Yet the same is true of the most sophisticated contemplative among the masters. All of us are "simple"; all that we can do in prayer is to return the letters of Creation to their source above.

III

The masters of Hasidic prayer, like most of their predecessors in the Jewish mystical tradition, were hesitant to write down any sort of systematic guide to the ways of contemplation. While they did have a clear sense (particularly in the school of the Maggid of Mezritsh) that there were specific ordered steps to be taken that could lead one up the devotional ladder, the composition of such a guide would have been a particular affront to their ideals of spontaneity and wholeness. By what steps in a manual can you guide a person to *hitlahavut*, that state where ecstasy fills the heart like a burning fire? Can any studied method really lead one to know that the soul is nothing but an outpouring of God's ever-flowing light?

Yet despite this lack of systematic introduction, the works of the early Hasidic masters are filled with hints as to the various rungs of inner prayer and how they are to be attained. From these references, scattered throughout early Hasidic literature, a composite picture of their approach to contemplative prayer can be reconstructed. It should be emphasized, however, that the following attempt at system-atization is not directly to be found in any single Hasidic source, but is rather culled from the advice of various masters in various situations of spiritual guidance.

There are two types of prayer-state generally described in Hasidic sources. *Katnut*, the "lesser" or ordinary state in which one generally begins to pray, is opposed to *gadlut*, the "greater" or expanded state of mystical consciousness. Prayer recited while in a state of *katnut* may contain within it great devotion; it is generally the simple giving of oneself to God and accepting the divine will. The prayer of *katnut* may contain both the love of God and awe before God's Presence, the two essential qualities for authentic prayer in Hasidism. In *katnut*, however, one is not transported beyond the self. Consciousness is not transformed and self-awareness is not tran-scended. I give myself to God in prayer, but I remain aware of the distinction between giver and receiver of this gift.

The ascent from this state to that of *gadlut* is one of the cen-tral themes of Hasidic prayer literature. While the simple devotions of the *katnut* state are highly valued, the true goal of the worshiper is to enter that world where "one may come to transcend time," where "distinctions between 'life' and 'death,' 'land' and 'sea,' have lost their meaning." The worshiper seeks to "concentrate so fully on prayer that one no longer is aware of the self ... to step outside the body's limits." Rapturous descriptions of the state of *gadlut* abound in Hasidic writings.

The first step in attainment of *gadlut* is the involvement of the entire self in the act of worship. There must be no reservations; you must not hold back any part of your self in prayer; the body is to be involved along with the soul in the act of worship: the rhythmic movement of the body, the sometimes loud outcry of the voice, the training of the eye to the page—all these externals are aids, in the first stages of prayer, to the involvement of the entire self.

As the ecstatic power of this involvement begins to over-whelm the worshiper, the externals, one by one, are set aside. The body will become still, the shout will become a whisper, and one may put the book aside and see the letters of prayer with the mind's eye alone. This "stripping off of the material world" in the act of prayer corresponds to the essential journey every person must make, according to Hasidic teaching, in the search for truth. The seeker has to shift his eye from external reality, where diversity and multiplicity seem to reign, to the inner truth, where nought but the ever-flowing *hiyyut*, or divine life, is real.

At this point, the winged ascent of the soul and word to the upper worlds begins in earnest. Prayer must ever be accompanied by the love and fear of God, the two emotions Jewish teachers had long seen as the "wings" that allow one's prayer to ascend to God. Each moment could become one of standing at Sinai, when the consuming love of God and total awe before God's tremendous power were most fully combined. As love and awe accompany the word upward, the letters become liberated from their verbal patterns and lead the soul back from the "World of Speech" to their higher source in the "World of Thought." Verbal prayer gives way to abstract contemplation, to a liberation of the worshiper's mind from all content other than the attachment to God. First all of one's energies are concentrated on the word as spoken with fullness; the word itself is released and nothing remains with the worshiper but the fullness of heart that, paradoxically, also marks one as an empty vessel ready to receive the light from above. Even the self-conscious feeling of this fullness must be transcended, for "a person who still knows how intensely he is praying has not yet overcome the awareness of self."

This description of the ascent from the verbal to the wholly contemplative state parallels the structure of the cosmos as depicted by the earlier Jewish esoteric tradition. The "World of Speech" is here identified with *shekhinah* (translated throughout this work as "Presence"), the last of the ten divine manifestations around which that tradition centers. *Shekhinah* is the Presence of God in the lower world, the indwelling glory of God that fills all of Creation. It is generally depicted by the mystics in feminine terms; the divinity that inhabits both world and soul longs to be reunited with her transcendent spouse. The "World of Thought" mentioned in these sources refers to *hokhmah* ("Wisdom," "Sophia"), the highest of the rungs according to Hasidic reckoning. The movement of the worshiper from speech to abstract thought is a journey of ascent through the realms of divine light, from one end of the cosmos to the other.

This emptying of the mind of all content, which Hasidic prayer shares with many other meditative techniques, finally leads to that place *within* God known as the "Nothing," or the realm of Primordial Nothingness. According to Kabbalistic theology, this Nothingness within God is the *ayin* or *nihil* out of which the world was created. All things are rooted in the divine "Nothing." As prayer ascends to God, the creative energy is returned to its source in the One. Creation, however, is viewed in Hasidism as a constant ongoing process: the world is ever pouring forth anew from this state of Nothingness, which lies at the innermost core of being. As the mind is emptied, the worshiper stands ready to be filled once again, having returned to that source from which Creation takes place.

Here one has reached the moment of ultimate transformation. In all change and growth, say the masters, the mysterious *ayin* is present. There is an ungraspable instant in the midst of all transformation when that which is about to be transformed is no longer what it had been until that moment, but has not yet emerged as its transformed self; that moment belongs to the *ayin* within God. Since change and transformation are *constant*, however, in fact all moments are moments of contact with the *ayin*, a contact that we are usually too blind to acknowledge. The height of contemplative prayer is seen as such a transforming moment, but one that is marked by a unique blend of awareness and self-transcendence. The worshiper is no longer a separate self but is fully absorbed, for that moment, in the Nothingness of divinity. That moment of absorption is transforming: the worshiper continues to recite the words of prayer but it is no longer the worshiper who speaks them. Rather it is the Presence who speaks through the one who prays. In that prayerful return to the source, we reach the highest human state, becoming nought but the passive instrument for the ever self-proclaiming praise of God.

IV

Any teaching that places such great emphasis on total concentration in prayer needs to deal with the question of distraction. What are we to do when "alien thoughts" enter the mind and lead us away from prayer? Sometimes it seems that the more intensely we try to concentrate, the more powerful and even sinful those thoughts become. How are we to be saved from seeing prayer become a battlefield in which distraction and self-castigation alternate to keep us far from God? Surely when we are busily punishing ourselves for the evil of wayward thoughts, we cannot have the joy and wholeness that are needed for God's service.

It is perhaps in response to this problem that the Ba'al Shem Tov's thought was most revolutionary. He spoke against the attempts of his contemporaries either to do battle with distracting thoughts or to see them as vanities that should simply be ignored. Just as he taught that each moment in life may be an opening to the Presence of God, he taught that each distraction in prayer may become a ladder by which to ascend to a new level of devotion. For one who truly believes that all things are from God and bear the Creator's mark can make no exception for the fantasies of his or her own mind! They too are from God and are sent to us as ways to God's service. The worshiper must break open the shell of evil surrounding the distracting thought, find the root of that thought in God, and join it to prayer. Thus a person who is distracted by sexual desire during worship should not seek to drive that desire from the mind, but rather should come to know that such desire itself is but a fallen spark from the World of Love, which seeks to be uplifted in the ascent of prayer. The thought needs to be "purified in its root," so that the energy animating it can be redeemed and brought back to God. When the Talmud states that a prayer leader who repeats his words and says, "Hear, hear, O Israel!" is to be silenced (probably for fear of dualistic heresy), the Ba'al Shem Tov comments:

> Why should the poor man be silenced? Perhaps when he said the first "Hear" he was distracted by some other thought, and he repeated the word only to pray

9

more devoutly. But that is the very root of dualism! In repeating the word, he is denying the legitimacy of his former prayer; he is denying that God was present in that moment of distraction! And only one who truly knows that God is present in all things, including those thoughts he seeks to flee, can be a leader of prayer.

Behind this matter lies the Ba'al Shem Tov's all-pervading commitment to the full integration of the self, a commitment that was not grasped by all of his disciples. The founder of Hasidism deeply believed that a person torn by inner struggles is not yet ready to come to God. Hence his comments denouncing excessive worry about minor sins. Brooding on our sinfulness, he taught, was merely a trick by the Evil One to keep us far from God. The service of God requires the deepest joy, and such joy cannot be experienced in a divided self. Repent of evil, know that God accepts your penitence in love, and return to serve with joy and wholeness.

V

Because Hasidic literature contains no systematic manual of contemplative prayer, the texts included in the present volume have been culled from many sources. A large number of them have been previously collected in such Hebrew anthologies as *Sefer Ba'al Shem Tov*, by Simeon Mendel Vednik of Gavarczow; *Romemut ha-Tefillah*, by Shlomo Rosenthal of Warsaw; and *Derekh Hasidim* by Nahman of Cheryn. In all cases, however, the translators have referred to the original sources of material, as indicated in the notes of this volume.

While the notes may be of some interest to students of Hasidism, the primary purpose of the present translation is devotional rather than academic. We offer these texts for the enrichment of the personal religious lives of our readers, for use as readings in the context of worship, and as a source of inspiration to those who seek to uncover the oneness of religious truth behind the garb of various mystical traditions. It is our belief that the authentic voice of Hasidic devotion, properly presented for the contemporary reader, may still speak to our spiritual situation.

We have taken great care, in translating these texts, not to reinterpret, but rather to allow the Hasidic masters to speak for themselves. Sometimes, however, rearrangement and condensing of the material was required. This is due to the nearly complete lack of concern for literary style on the part of the Hasidic authors and editors. The theoretical literature of Hasidism, in which the prayer instruction texts are often to be found, is poorly edited, often repetitive, and sometimes based upon garbled notes in Hebrew summarizing longer sermons that were preached in Yiddish. As such, they at times require some structural rewording when presented in translation, which necessarily involves an attempt to return them, in the translator's mind, to their original oral form and context.

Since this translation was undertaken primarily for devotional purposes, we have sought to avoid use of the third person masculine gender. Such avoidance was not possible in all cases. It is fully the translators' intent that all readers, women as well as men, non-Jews as well as Jews, should have access to the authentic sources of Hasidism.

The sources of this collection are the teachings of the Ba'al Shem Tov, the Maggid Dov Baer of Mezritsh, and their immediate disciples, in the latter part of the eighteenth century. Works of such particular Hasidic schools as HaBaD and Bratslav, which differ quite radically both in style and content from these teachings, have not been included.

It should be emphasized that the texts found in this volume did not originate in abstract thought. Many were undoubtedly said to disciples who came to their masters with particular problems in their prayer lives. They belong to moments that can only be re-created in the imagination of the reader. Similarly, this translation is intended for use. Hopefully it will speak to particular moments, touch particular lives. This offering is an attempt to make a modest contribution to the rebirth of religious life, nurtured by the sources of Jewish prayer and the wisdom of its greatest masters.

The Power of Your Prayer

What a great wonder that we should be able to
    draw so near to God in prayer.
How many walls there are between God and human beings!
Even though God fills all the world,
    God is so very hidden!
Yet a single word of prayer can topple all the walls
    and bring you close to God.[1]

When a Jew speaks a word of prayer
  in love and awe,
    the power of that word gives birth
    to God's glory.
The angels call out to God:
    "Who is like Your Israel,
    a unique people in the world!"
How great is even a single word of such prayer:
    it causes all the angels to sing to God!
All the worlds join with the one who serves the Lord.

This is the meaning of "The Song of Songs"—
    one who sings a song below can
    arouse many songs on high![2]

The prophet says: "Speak unto the heart of Jerusalem,
    and call out to her that her host is fully present."
The word *'al,* used for "unto" in this verse,
    can also mean "with."
Speak your words of Torah and prayer
    with your heart, which is called "Jerusalem."
In this way you "call to her."

All of your calling out and prayer should be to her,
    to *shekhinah,*
        the Jerusalem that is the gateway of prayer.
Of this Scripture says:
    "Let them pray to You through their land."
All prayers have to go up through the gateway that faces
        Jerusalem.
    But only those prayers that come *from* Jerusalem,
    that of the heart, can reach this gateway of Jerusalem.
By speaking the words with the heart's Jerusalem,
    you enable them to "call out to her,"
    and to arrive at this gateway of Jerusalem.
"Her host is fully present," for now this prayer is full
    and perfect in all its words and letters, who are her hosts.[3]

Once a wise man was asked: "On what thought do
    you concentrate as you pray?"
He replied: "I bind myself to the Divine Life
    that flows through all of God's creations.
    As I join myself to each
    I seek to bring the life within it back to God."
"Destroyer!" said the other. "How can the world
    exist if you draw out all its life?"
The wise man remained unperturbed:
    "Do you really think I can do all that—
    I who have so little power?"
"But in that case," replied the other,
    "of what value is your prayer?"

The truth is that you must believe
    in the power of your prayer.
The truly wise, who stand before the King in prayer,
    surely can bind themselves to the flow of Life.
But they are not allowed to do so always—
    lest by their uplifting powers
    they do indeed destroy the world.[4]

It is possible to be so humble
    that your very humility
    keeps you far from God.
Humble people may not believe that their own
         prayers
    can cause the Presence
    to flow through all the worlds.
But how then can you believe
    that even angels are nourished
    by your words?

Know the power of your prayer
    and serve your God in fullness![5]

Why do the prayers of the righteous at times
      seem to go unanswered?

There is a king who has two sons.
Each of them comes to receive his gift
      from the royal table.
The first son appears at his father's doorway,
      and as soon as he is seen, his request is granted.
The father holds this son in low esteem
      and is annoyed by his presence.
The king orders that the gifts be handed
      to his son at the door
      so that he will not approach the table.

Then the king's
      beloved son appears.
The father takes great pleasure in this son's arrival
      and does not want him to leave too quickly.
For this reason the king delays granting his request,
      hoping that the son will then draw near to him.
As the son comes closer,
      he feels his father's love so deeply
      that he does not hesitate to stretch forth
      his own hand to the royal table.

Both of the sons receive
      what they had sought from their father;
      the portions in themselves are no different.
But the first son receives his gifts in shame,
      seeing that his father stays so far from him.
His brother, however, has come so close to the king
      that he himself can take that which he needs.[6]

"Who can give word to the powers of Y-H-W-H,
 causing all His praise to be heard?"
How is it possible that so lowly a physical being as a human
 could stand up and praise the Lord of all?
God is so holy that not even an angel or a seraph could praise
  Him!
But therein lies the answer.
If there were any being that were capable of truly praising God,
 it would stand to reason that only such a one and no
 other should do so.
But that is not the case regarding God's service.
There is no creature either above or below
 who can really declare His praises!
In that case, *all* can "cause His praises to be heard,"
 even the lowliest of God's creatures.
If none of us can fully do it, all of us can.[7]

Of communal prayer it has been told:

Once in a tropical country, a certain splendid bird,
    more colorful than any that had ever been seen,
    was sighted at the top of the tallest tree.
The bird's plumage contained within it
    all the colors in the world.
But the bird was perched so high
    that no single person
    could ever hope to reach it.

When news of the bird reached the ears of the king,
    he ordered that a number of his subjects
    try to bring the bird to him.
They were to stand on one another's shoulders
    until the highest one could reach the bird
    and bring it to the king.
The people assembled near the tree,
    but while they were standing
    balanced on one another's shoulders,
    some of those near the bottom
    decided to wander off.
As soon as the first one moved,
    the entire chain collapsed,
    injuring several of them.
Still the bird remained uncaptured.

The people had doubly failed the king.
For even greater than his desire to see the bird
    was his wish to see his people
    so closely joined to one another.[8]

"For people to comprise a quorum for prayer,
They all need to be in one place along with their prayer leader."

But if ten people are gathered in a synagogue,
    each asking for their own needs,
    they are to be considered "scattered,"
    even though they are in the same building.

One has turned his thoughts to his vineyard,
    another to his olive grove.
One may be praying for his own life,
    while another thinks of his children—or whatever else.
The essence of prayer is not like that.
All ten need to be "in one place"—
    directing themselves toward the Cosmic One,
    praying that He and His name will be one,
    that God's kingdom will soon be revealed to us.

If their prayer leader is with them in this
    then what is hinted at in King Solomon's words—
    "You will hear, O heaven!"—
    will come to pass,
    since the words "heaven" and "prayer leader"
    have the same numerical equivalent in Hebrew.

The prayer leader serves as the intermediary
    who presents our words to the Ruler of the Universe.
The essence of prayer is to complete God's kingdom on earth.[9]

When our sages describe a leader of prayer,
    sometimes they speak of "one who goes down in front of
       the ark"
    and sometimes "one who passes before the ark."

The *tsaddik* who prays to God has to become attached to the
            words of prayer.
It is the holy words themselves that take the lead.
But there are some great *tsaddikim*
    who are on a higher rung than this: they lead the words.
This was the rung of Moses,
    who was "husband" of the *shekhinah*,
    according to the holy *Zohar*.

If one "goes down before the ark,"
    it is the word that is leading:
    the person praying stands "beneath" the word.
But the one who "passes before the ark"
    is leading the word, standing above it.[10]

Preparing
the
Way

Faith is the basis of all worship;
  only the truly faithful can pray each day.
And what is the basis of faith?
  "God renews each day the work of Creation."
The faithful one sees
  that every day is a new Creation,
  that all the worlds are new,
  that we ourselves have just been born.
How could we not want to sing
  the praise of the Creator?

If we do not have the faith
  that God creates anew each day,
  prayer becomes an old, unwanted habit.
How difficult it is to say
  the same words day after day!
Thus Scripture says: "Cast us not into old age!"—
  may the word never become old for us.[11]

Take special care to guard your tongue
    before the morning prayer.
Even greeting your fellow, we are told,
    can be harmful at that hour.
A person who wakes up in the morning is
    like a new creation.
Begin your day with unkind words,
    or even trivial matters—
        even though you may later turn to prayer,
        you have not been true to your Creation.
All of your words each day
    are related to one another.
All of them are rooted
    in the first words that you speak.[12]

No matter what the season,
    take special care
    to begin your prayer before sunrise.
Most of the service should be completed
    before the sun appears.
The great difference between prayer at dawn
    and prayer recited later in the day
    can hardly be imagined.
Before dawn one can still combat
    the destructive forces of the coming day.
But once the sun is out upon the earth,
    "nothing is hidden from its heat."
Do not consider this a small thing,
    for the Master himself
    took such great care in this matter
    that he would even worship without a quorum
    in order to say his prayers at the proper hour.[13]

A person of spirit may begin to pray
    in awe and trembling,
    saying:
    "Who am I, a poor clod of earth,
    to stand before the King of kings in prayer?"

The person speaks only a partial truth,
    not yet knowing the higher truth,
    that all things, even the material world,
    are filled with God's presence.
Indeed such a person cannot speak the words of prayer—
    better that he remain silent before the Lord.

Thus Scripture says:
    "God is in heaven and you are upon the earth;
    do not rush to speak, and let your words be few."
As long as you believe that God is only in heaven
    and does not fill the earth—
    let your words be few.
Only when you come to know
    that you too contain God's Presence—
    only then can you begin to pray.[14]

How much more pleasing to God is prayer in joy
    than that which is said in sadness and tears!
A poor man begs and weeps
        as he comes before the king;
        he can be dismissed with but a trifle.
But when a noble prince steps forward,
        the king's praises joyfully on his lips,
        and then asks some favor,
        he cannot be treated so lightly.
To him the king grants his greatest gifts—
        a prince must receive a princely portion.[15]

Before you begin to pray,
    decide that you are ready to die
    in that very prayer.
There are some people so intense in their worship,
    who give up so much of their strength to prayer,
    that if not for a miracle they would die
    after uttering only two or three words.
It is only through God's great kindness
    that such people live,
    that their soul does not leave them
    as they are joined to Him in prayer.[16]

There are times when you must prepare yourself
    before you can pray.
Reciting Psalms or studying Torah before prayer
    may provide the strength you need.
But take care also to avoid giving yourself too fully
    to these preparations,
        lest they consume all your strength
        and leave no room for prayer itself.[17]

Enter into prayer slowly.
Do not exhaust your strength,
    but proceed step by step.
Even if you are not aroused as your prayer begins,
    give close attention to the words you speak.
As you grow in strength
    and God helps you to draw near,
    you can even say the words more quickly
    and remain in God's Presence.[18]

"Prepare yourself in the entranceway,
    so that you may enter the palace."

When you begin to pray,
    you are still in that entranceway,
    the place where you prepare yourself
    to enter the courtyard of the King.
Standing before the King brings forth great awe,
    much more than you previously had.
When you begin to prepare yourself,
    you lack that sense of awe,
    but you feel it greatly
    once you come inside
    and are in the King's presence.

There are many levels to this.
You do not feel the same awe before a high official that you
        do before a king.
A king of kings, an emperor, brings you to an even greater
        state.

So too is it above.
"One guard higher than the next."
Yes, prepare yourself first in that entranceway,
    so that you may enter.
But once you are in the palace,
    understand that there exist rungs after rungs.
"Know before whom you stand" on level after level,
    each higher than the previous one.
There is always a level of awe that you have not yet attained.
You may ascend from "king" to "king of kings,"
    but this goes on forever.[19]

The evil urge has two ways
    of keeping you from prayer;
To each there is an appropriate response.

At times its voice will say to you:
    "Who are you
      that you dare come into this holy place
      to speak before the Lord?
      How dare you pray—you of unclean lips,
      you who are so filled with sin!"
If you hear these words, reply:
    "See all the good I have done!
    See the way I have kept the Lord's commandments,
    how much joy I have brought Him with my prayer!"

But even your reply can become an opening
    for the voice of evil.
For the evil urge can also dress itself
    in pride and say:
    "You are the leader of all Israel,
    the greatest of all!
    Surely humility is no virtue
    for one so great as you.
    What a great scholar you are!
    How carefully you fulfill God's commands!"
Know then that this too is the trap
    of the evil one and say:
    "How great are my sins! How empty my
      devotion!
    I have not fulfilled
    even a single one of God's commands!"[20]

There are many people who turn
    the words of prayer into songs.
They even go so far as to plan out
    their worship, saying:
        "Here I will sing this melody; there, another."
They call this the service of God and hope to reach
    states of ecstasy by such song.
They even believe
    that God is pleased by such worship!
What fools they are—
    they walk in darkness
    and have not seen the truth.

A person who is truly at prayer
    must seek to go beyond the material world.
Speak the words simply,
    and devote all your attention
    to the holy letters
    and to the meaning of your prayer.
It is this true devotion
    that will bring you to the love and fear of God—
    and will really set your heart aflame.[21]

Meet God in the Word

"Make yourself an ark of gopher wood
… make a window for the ark
and finish it to a cubit above;
and set the door of the ark in its side;
make it with lower, second, and third decks.
… Go into the ark,
you and all your household…."

The ark of Noah is the word of prayer.
"Make yourself a window for the ark":
Let the words of prayer
be a window through which
you see to the ends of the earth.
The window is the "light" in the ark
which is the word: Speak the word
in such a way
that the inner light shines through it.

"Make it with lower, second, and third decks."
Each letter contains worlds and souls
and the Presence of God.
As the letters are joined to one another
and form the words of prayer,
all that is within them
rises up to God.
One who joins his soul
to this process
brings all the worlds together in boundless joy.

"Go into the ark,
you and all your household"
—enter into the word
with all your body,
with all your strength.[22]

How does a person come to know God's hidden
    ways?

The stars, which by day are not visible,
    can nevertheless be seen
    by one who uses a proper lens.
The holy letters of prayer form such lenses;
    they may be used as telescopes for seeing into
    the hidden ways of God.
One who has already transcended the self
    and has come to know
    that he is nothing—
    such a person can look so deeply
    into the letters
    that the divine qualities of which they speak
    become real to him.
As one says "the great" during prayer,
    the greatness of God appears
    in those very letters.
Thus one sees the power of God
    in the words "the powerful,"
    the awe of God in the words "the awesome."
The letters themselves have the power
    to draw forth these qualities from above.

It is through the letters
    that the word of God
    may come to dwell with us.[23]

Think that the letters of prayer
    are the garments of God.
What a joy to be making a garment
    for the greatest of kings!
Enter into every letter with all your strength.
God dwells within each letter;
    as you enter it, you become one with God.[24]

See your prayer as arousing the letters
    through which heaven and earth
    and all living things were created.
The letters are the life of all;
    when you pray through them,
    all Creation joins with you in prayer.
All that is around you can be uplifted;
    even the song of a passing bird
    may enter into such a prayer.[25]

Put all your strength into the words,
    proceeding from letter to letter
    with such concentration
    that you lose awareness of your bodily self.
It will then seem that the letters themselves
    are flowing into one another.
This uniting of the letters is one's greatest joy.
If joy is felt as two human bodies come together,
    how much greater must be the joy
    of this union in spirit![26]

Know that each word of prayer is a complete self.
If all of your strength is not in it,
    it is born incomplete,
    like one lacking a limb.[27]

When you focus all your thought
    on the power of the words,
      you may begin to see the sparks of light
      that shine within them.
The sacred letters are the chambers
    into which God pours flowing light.
The lights within each letter, as they touch,
    ignite one another,
      and new lights are born.

It is of this the Psalmist says:
    "Light is sown for the righteous,
    and joy for the upright in heart."[28]

"With the Lord your God"
God is present in the words of Torah.
Enter into the words,
    speaking them with all your strength.
Your soul will then meet God in the word—
    the soul that is itself a part of God above.

This is the true union of the blessed Holy One,
    and His Presence, of which the mystics speak.
"With the Lord your God"—with the Lord, your God—
    the Presence within you, your God,
    is joined together with "the Lord"—
    its eternal source.[29]

If prayer is pure and untainted,
 surely that holy breath
 that rises from your lips
 will join with the breath of heaven
 that is always flowing
 into you from above.
Thus our masters have taught the verse
 "Every breath shall praise God":
 with every single breath that you breathe,
 God is praised.
As the breath leaves you, it ascends to God,
 and then it returns to you from above.
Thus that part of God
 that is within you
 is reunited with its source.[30]

The purpose of all prayer is to uplift the words,
 to return them to their source above.
Just as the world was created
 by the downward flow of letters,
Our task is to form those letters into words
 and take them back to God.
If you come to know this dual process,
 your prayer may be joined
 to the constant flow of Creation—
 word to word, voice to voice,
 breath to breath, thought to thought.

The words fly upward and come before Him.
As God turns to look at the ascending word,
 life flows through all the worlds
 and prayer receives its answer.
This looking is itself a sort of flow downward,
 reaffirming the existence of all the worlds.
All this happens in an instant
 and all this happens continually;
Time has no meaning in the sight of God.
The divine wellspring gushes forth in each instant.
The flow is constant,
 and its nature is to do good
 and give blessing to God's creatures.

But if you pray or study in this way
 you may become a channel for that spring,
bringing its blessing and goodness to the entire world.[31]

When a person prays in an ordinary way,
    the words of prayer have no life of their own.
It is only the name of God appearing in their midst
    that gives them life.
Thus when you recite the words:
    "Blessed art Thou, O Lord ...,"
    life does not enter the words
    until the word "Lord" is uttered.
But when a true master of prayer recites the words
    every word is a name of God.
"Blessed" is a name, "Thou" is a name....[32]

Do not think that the words of prayer
    as you say them
    go up to God.
It is not the words themselves that ascend;
    it is rather the burning desire of your heart
    that rises like smoke toward heaven.
If your prayer consists only of words and letters,
    and does not contain your heart's desire—
    how can it rise up to God?[33]

I heard from my teacher a comment on
  "Whoever sets a fixed place for his prayer,
  the God of Abraham helps him."

When one speaks the prayers without awareness,
  the letters do not cleave to their Root.
Rather, they remain in the lower world,
  that of the spheres.
All the firmaments are within that world of spheres.
When the letters are attached to those firmaments
  that are constantly swirling about,
  the letters swirl with them.

But if you make the letters cleave to the blessed Creator,
  who is above those spheres,
  you are "setting a fixed place for your prayers."
You are firmly "fixed" on God.
Then indeed "the God of Abraham helps" you.[34]

Beyond
the Walls
of Self

"Go out of the ark,
        you and your wife and your children."
Take *yourself* out of the words of your prayer.
Let your prayer not be for yourself
        or for your household,
        but only for the sake of God and His Presence.[35]

A person should be so absorbed in prayer
    that he is no longer
    aware of his own self.
There is nothing for him but the flow of Life;
    all his thoughts are with God.
He who still knows how intensely he is praying
    has not yet overcome the bonds of self.[36]

You must forget yourself in prayer.
Think of yourself as nothing
  and pray only for the sake of God.
In such prayer you may come to transcend time,
  entering the highest realms
  of the World of Thought.
There all things are as one;
Distinctions between "life" and "death,"
  "land" and "sea,"
  have lost their meaning.
But none of this can happen
  as long as you remain attached
  to the reality of the material world.
Here you are bound to the distinctions
  between good and evil
  that emerge only in the lower realms of God.
How can one who remains attached to his own self
  go beyond time to the world where all is one?[37]

The human body is always finite;
It is the spirit that is boundless.
Before you begin to pray,
    cast aside that which limits you
    and enter the endless world of Nothing.
In prayer turn to God alone
    and have no thoughts of yourself at all.
Nothing but God exists for you;
    you yourself have ceased to be.
The true redemption of the soul can only happen
    as you step outside the body's limits.[38]

In prayer seek to make yourself into a vessel
    for God's Presence.
God, however, is without limit;
"Endless" is God's name.
How can any finite vessel hope to contain
    the endless God?
Therefore, see yourself as nothing:
    only one who is nothing
    can contain the fullness
    of the Presence.[39]

As long as you can still say the words
  "Blessed art Thou"
  by your own will,
    know that you have not yet reached
    the deeper levels of prayer.
Be so stripped of selfhood that you have
    neither the awareness
    nor the power
to say a single word on your own.[40]

Why are we told to recite the verse
    "O Lord, open my lips
    and let my mouth declare Your praise"
    before our most sacred prayer?
Like banks to a river,
    lips form the outer edges of human speech.
We pray that God may release us from those limits,
    so that our mouths may declare
    God's endless praise.[41]

As a person begins to pray, reciting the words:
 "O Lord, open my lips
  and let my mouth declare Your praise,"
  the Presence of God comes into him.
Then it is the Presence herself
  who commands his voice;
  it is she who speaks the words through him.
One who knows in faith
  that all this happens within him
  will be overcome with trembling
  and with awe.[42]

There are times when the love of God
   burns so powerfully within your heart
   that the words of prayer seem to rush forth,
   quickly and without deliberation.
At such times it is not you yourself who speak;
   rather it is through you
   that the words are spoken.[43]

When you speak, think that the World of Speech is
    at work within you,
      for without that presence,
      you would not be able to speak at all.
Similarly, you would not think at all were it not
    for the World of Thought within you.
A person is like a ram's horn;
    the only sound you make is
    that which is blown through you.
Were there no one blowing into the horn,
    there would be no sound at all.[44]

There are two rungs of service
    that a person can come to know.
The first is called *katnut*, "the lesser service."
In this state you may know
    that there are many heavens encircling you,
    that the earth on which you stand is
    but a tiny point,
    and that all the world is nothing
    before the Endless God—
    but even knowing all these things,
    you yourself cannot ascend.
This is still the "lesser" service.
It is of this state the prophet says:
    "From afar God appears to me."

But when you serve in *gadlut*, "the greater service,"
    you take hold of yourself with all your strength
    and your mind soars upward,
    breaking through the heavens all at once,
    rising higher,
    higher than the angels.[45]

There are times when you are praying
    in an ordinary state of mind
    and you feel that you cannot draw near to God.
But then in an instant
    the light of your soul will be kindled
    and you will go up to the highest worlds.
You are like one who has been given a ladder:
The light that shines in you is a gift from above.[46]

Our sages said that prayer has to be offered with the mind of
      Jacob.
"The voice is the voice of Jacob."
They speak of "little Jacob," and he represents humility.

All of prayer seeks to draw forth bounty
      from the Source of desire,
      bringing it down from world to world.

As it traverses each of those worlds,
      it has to keep contracting itself,
      coming closer to corporeality
      at each stage in the journey.
Only because it keeps reducing itself
      can that infinite stream of light
      enter this physical and limited world.
It is indeed a wonder that we lowly mortal creatures
      can take in such a pure and brilliant light.

All the divine attributes are found in the human being as well.
We are able to attach ourselves to our Creator
      in prayer and acts of worship
      only when we too contract ourselves
      and make ourselves smaller.

If we consider ourselves large,
      that same largeness will be awakened above,
      making it impossible for bounty to enter the world.
"God despises all those of haughty heart."
God is not present in the prayers
      of those who think highly of themselves,
      the very opposite of what God wants.

That is why my teacher said that a person is like a mirror.
Whatever self you present to it
      is reflected back to you from above.
If you present bigness,
      you will arouse the same,
      and no light will come into the world.[47]

There are times
    when your love for God is so powerful
    that you offer your very life,
    putting all your strength into words,
    paying no heed to your bodily needs.

Even if your very soul pours out of you as you speak,
    you give yourself entirely to God
    for the sake of God's holiness.

This is because the Creator has blessed you
    with an abundance of awareness
    with which to serve Him.
Do not consider it your own achievement.
Without this divine gift of greater awareness,
    you would not be giving this offering.

This is the meaning of the verse
"If a person gives all the wealth of his household for love,
    they will surely shower upon him."
As you begin to pray and to serve God,
    the blessed Holy One
    gives you this gift of greater awareness,
    leading you to long and desire to serve even more.

"If a person gives all the wealth of his household"
    refers to the strength you put forth in loving God.
Know that this is not due to your own goodness,
    but is being showered upon you from heaven.
You are being given a gift.[48]

The person is a throne
upon which Y-H-W-H is seated,
as Scripture says: "I will dwell among them."

It is not proper to have the King seated on a damaged throne,
only a whole one.
The people Israel are God's throne and chariot.
But now "the throne is not whole" due to sin.

Aleph is missing from the Hebrew word *kisse* [throne].
This is the cosmic *Aleph*, the One.
It does not befit His glory to be seated on a damaged throne.
Nevertheless, He dwells with us always—
but in an incomplete way.
All we are asking for in seeking forgiveness
is that we be able to serve as a throne for Y-H-W-H,
that He dwell below
and "the whole earth be filled with His glory...."
Then both throne and name will be complete.

The whole battle with Amalek is the struggle with the evil urge;
it is because of sins that the throne is not complete.
Have no intent for your own self,
but only for the sake of glorious Y-H-W-H,
who desires to dwell below,
so that you can be a chariot for Him,
making His name great.

This is what Moses meant in saying
"As I call upon the name Y-H-W-H,
give greatness to our God."

When I call out,
my whole intent is that the name become whole.
You too do the same:
"Give"—prepare yourselves to bring
"greatness to our God."
"Israel gives strength to God,"
making His name great.[49]

Pain hurts us because the whole person is joined together as
    one.
If you bang your finger,
    your whole self feels the pain,
    since you are a single person.
The same is true of emotional pain.

But this is no longer the case
    if you connect yourself to something else
    in a total way.
Then you lose that prior attachment
    to your own body or emotions.
You don't feel anything that happens to you
    back in that prior place.
That connection has already been replaced
    by your new attachment.
In this way it is possible
    to detach your entire person
    from any sort of pain,
    all of which is caused by attachment,
    whether for good or for ill.

When you enter entirely into some holy matter,
    be it a *mitsvah*, Torah study, or prayer,
    with such great attachment
    that you no longer feel anything of your prior material
    self,
    you have "removed the soiled garments
    and dressed in robes of strength."
You become garbed in the spirit of holiness.

When you dress yourself
    in the words of Torah or prayer,
    as in "Come in, you and all your household,
    to the word,"
    putting all your attention into them

and negating all your former feelings,
    you are in a state of complete oneness with God.

The garb of the *mitsvot* surrounds you,
    and God is within them.
Thus you are united with God
    without any interruption,
        as in "Spread your wing over your maidservant."
It is the shared garment that unites you,
    since Torah and *mitsvot* are divinity itself, as is known.
As you enter them,
    you unite with God,
    and taste something of the World to Come.

This is the meaning of
"Those who have tasted of her have attained life."
One cannot cleave to life
    and the supernal light in the World to Come
    without having tasted of it in this world.
That is lacking for those
    who live the life of Torah and commandments
    only by rote,
    without that sense of intense attachment.[50]

Prayer
for the
Sake of Heaven

All of your prayers should be
      for the sake of the Presence,
      who herself is called prayer.
Each of your needs is only a reflection
      of some lack in the Presence.
Pray for her fulfillment,
      not merely your own.
As you bring oneness to the upper worlds
      and restore that which is lacking above,
      your own needs too will be fulfilled.
All the wonders that the Master performed—
      healing the sick and dying,
      opening the eyes of the blind,
      restoring the wellsprings gone dry,
      helping the barren to conceive,
      great miracles that the world had not seen
      since the days of Hanina ben Dosa—
All this came about because our Master thought
      only of that which was lacking above.
"There is no place without Him"—
      every deed you do is a dwelling-place for God.[51]

Maimonides says in his credo:
   "One should pray to Him alone;
   to no one else should he pray."
But the text can also be read:
   "One should pray for Him alone;
   for nothing else should he pray."
The purpose of Creation is only that we pray for God.
Material things, this world—
   such nonsense is not worthy of prayer.[52]

The Psalmist says:
   "A prayer of a poor man"—
But the text may also read:
   "A prayer to a poor man!"

Though the treasure houses of the king are full,
   they are managed by the king's officials.
Having nothing to do with all his treasures,
   the king himself is like a poor man.

One who comes in search of treasure
   will never see the King.
Only one who seeks no riches,
   who prays as to a poor man,
   can come before the King Himself.[53]

"If the man is poor, you may not lie down with his
        loan-pledge
    [i.e., delay overnight the return of his clothing held on
        pledge],
    since it is what clothes his body.
In what will he wrap himself?"

The meaning of this verse is that all prayers
    are wrapped up in the prayers of the poor.
As it is written: "True sacrifice to God is a broken spirit."
The essence of prayer is to stand with a broken heart
    for God's destroyed palace and scattered children.

There remains no way to worship other than worship of the
        heart,
    as we seek to raise up the *shekhinah*
    and unite her with her Beloved.
Such prayer is a wrapping or garment for all the others.

This is not true of the one who enters a synagogue
    to pray for worldly needs.
Even though he prays out of faith that God
    can truly provide all the good he desires,
    this prayer is not for the sake of his Creator.
He is acting more like the lender,
    seeking to take back his pledge garment.

But the verse says that "you may not lie down with his
        loan-pledge,"
    meaning that the one who seeks to take back the pledge
    [to receive something in exchange for his prayer]
    will not permit the "lying down"—
    the act of union between *shekhinah* and her Beloved.

Rather he will find himself "standing outside"
    not within the *shekhinah*, but outside her.[54]

80

Prayer for the Sake of Heaven

"Do not be like those who serve the master
    in order to receive a reward.
    Be rather like those who serve the master
    not in order to receive a reward."
But another version of this text reads:
    "… serve the master
    in order not to receive a reward!"
Both versions are correct, but the latter
    speaks of a higher rung of service.

The first version surely speaks
    of a proper kind of prayer,
    one in which the worshiper
    directs his thoughts only
    to the needs of God.
It matters little to him
    whether his own personal petition
    is granted or denied.
All of this servant's deeds
    are for the sake of heaven.

But there is yet a higher rung,
    of which the second version speaks.
There is a man who lives with a burning desire
    to speak with the king.
The king has issued a decree that anyone
    who comes forward with a petition
    shall have his wish granted.
This man, however, longs only
    to stand before the king
    and speak with him always.
In him the king's decree arouses only fear:
    whatever he asks, the king will grant,
    and no longer will he be able to speak with him!
He would rather his petition not be granted,
    so that he might have reason always

to return to the presence of the king.
This man serves "in order
    not to receive a reward."

This is the meaning of:
    "A prayer of a poor man who is faint,
    pouring forth his words before the Lord."
This poor man seeks nothing more in prayer
    than that his words pour forth before the Lord.[55]

The liturgy prescribes that
    the Prayer of Love must be recited
    before the Proclamation of God's Oneness.
The Master was told that the Messiah has not come
    because people do not
    devote themselves sufficiently to this prayer.
These words of love are the kisses
    that precede sexual union,
    awakening desire in the Presence
    so that her child, compassion,
    might come forth.[56]

Do not rush through your weekday prayers thinking:
 "On the Sabbath I will pray with spirit."
In such prayer you would be like the king's servant
  who seems deeply attached to his tasks
  only as long as the king
  stands before him, but loses his devotion
  when the king is not in view.
This is not a faithful servant.

If you truly want to serve, know in faith
  that there is no good
  for you in life without the King.
Serve always as you do
  when the King stands before you.[57]

To those beset by suffering,
    the following has been told:
There was a man who had a young child.
At times the father sought to frighten the boy.
He would dress up in strange clothing
    so that his son would not know him.
At first the child was frightened,
      but as time passed he came to know
      that this too was his father.
Then he would call out, "Father!"
      and the father, filled with compassion,
      would take off the disguise
      and reveal himself to his son.

So it is with those who suffer.
When they come to understand
      that it is God Himself
      who is the source of their pain,
      they can then begin to call out to Him.
But those who do not see that all is from God
      and seek their cure elsewhere—
      these will never find true healing.[58]

In God's
Presence

"Pour out your heart like water
in the Presence of the Lord."

On the second day of Creation,
God separated the upper and lower waters.
At the moment of their separation, we are told,
the lower waters cried out:
"We too long to be near our Creator!"
So it is with the soul:
it too once dwelt in the upper realms,
near to God,
and has fallen to the lowest depths.
Like the lower waters of Creation,
it cries out to return to God.
"Pour out your heart like the waters,"
longing again to be
"in the Presence of the Lord."[59]

We are told that God's name as it is spoken means
      that God is Lord of all.
But the Name as written is that of God beyond:
      He who was and is and will be,
      the source of life for all the worlds.
The very letters of this Name are themselves
      the source of life.

When those of understanding heart begin to pray
      and come upon the Name,
      they see all this before them.
Can there be a greater joy than speaking face-to-face
      with the Eternal King, the life of every soul?
Of such moments Scripture says:
      "Let Him kiss me with the kisses of His mouth."[60]

P rayer is union with the Divine Presence.
Just as two people will move their bodies
      back and forth as they begin the act of love,
      so must a person accompany
      the beginning of prayer
      with the rhythmic swaying of the body.
But as one reaches the heights of union
      with the Presence,
      the movement of the body ceases.[61]

Be joyful always.
Know that God's Presence is with you,
      that you are looking directly at your Creator
      and your Creator at you.
Know that the Creator can do all that He desires:
      that in an instant
He could destroy all the worlds,
      and in an instant renew them.
In Him are rooted all powers, both good and harmful;
His flowing life is everywhere.
Only Him do I trust!
Only Him do I fear![62]

What is *devekut*, or attachment to God,
    of which the masters speak?

Some say that it is a holding fast to each word—
    attachment to each word is so great
    that one cannot bear to part with it.

But others say that this attachment comes to one
    who truly fulfills God's commands—
    making the body a throne for the mind,
    the mind a throne for the spirit,
    and the spirit a throne for the soul.

Then the soul too becomes a throne
    for the light of the Presence
    that rests upon you.
The light spreads forth around you,
    and you, at the center of that light,
    tremble in your joy.[63]

"When God is seated upon His throne,
  a fire of silence falls upon
  the heavenly beings."
When a person says the words of prayer
   so that they become a throne for God
   an awesome silent fire takes hold of him.
Then he knows not where he is;
  he cannot see, he cannot hear.
All this happens in the flash of an instant—
   as he ascends beyond the world of time.[64]

It is possible to pray in such a way
  that no other person
  can know of your devotion.
Though you make no movement of your body,
  your soul is all aflame within you,
And when you cry out in the ecstasy of that moment—
  your cry will be a whisper.[65]

There are times when a person's body
    may remain completely still
    while the soul serves God in silent prayer.
In such moments your prayer may be filled
    with a burning and awesome love,
    though one who sees you
    might never guess the depth
    of your inner service.
Only those who are already at one with God
    may attain this prayer
    of inner flame and outer stillness.
Such worship has greater power
    than devotion that can be seen by others.
The "shells" of evil that feed upon wayward prayers
    cannot reach this silent prayer,
    for it is deeply hidden within the self.[66]

Learn to pray quietly;
     even God's praises should be recited
     in a low voice.
Your shouts should be whispers.
But even so, say the words with all your strength,
     as it is written:
     "All my bones shall say: 'O Lord, who is like You!'"
Those who truly cleave to God—
     their outcry is a whisper.[67]

A person may come to sense two kinds of movement
     taking place within him during prayer.
At times you may feel the left hand of God
          pushing you away;
          at other times God's right hand draws you near.
But even as you are pushed away,
          know still
          that this is only for the sake of your return.
Even as you feel
          the might of God's left hand upon you,
          see that it is God Himself
          who touches you.
This too accept in love,
          and, trembling, kiss the hand that pushes you—
          for in that very moment,
          the right hand awaits your coming near.[68]

Our sages have taught that the word "standing" [*'amidah*]
    always refers to prayer,
    as in "Pinhas stood up and prayed."

This is hard to understand.
Do people really not stand up except to pray?

This must be referring to some matter of the mind
    rather than what it seems to say.
In fact our sages were not talking here about ordinary people,
    but only about those who have perfected
    the fear of God and Torah.
Of these they properly said that all of their "standing" is prayer.
Such people's minds are always in motion,
    walking higher and higher
    from rung to rung,
    from world to world.

A person who seeks God, wanting to serve truly
    and be attached to God,
    has to be seeking day and night.
You do this through Torah and *mitsvot*,
    by joining together holy letters and words,
    by beseeching the holy angels of each world and rung.

You cannot stand in one perfect spot.
That is why the righteous are called "walkers."
One cannot imagine them standing still except in prayer.
"Prayer" here means absolute cleaving and attachment to the
        blessed Creator.
The same is true of our daily prayer.

We walk through all the worlds,
    singing and blessing our way
    through the verses of Psalms that open the service.
We keep reaching higher levels

as we go through the service,
 even though we are not yet speaking directly to the King
 and are not yet fully attached.
Only when we reach the *'amidah* are we there
 with no interruption, curtain, or space,
 even of that which is holy,
 between us and God.
There is nothing but the simple endless Light.

That is why this world is called *'atsilut*, from *'etsel*, or "next to."
The person, as it were, stands truly next to Y-H-W-H.
This refers to the eighteen benedictions,
 when you stand in the world of *'atsilut*,
 with no curtain or space dividing you from your Maker.

The endless Light surrounds you from all sides
 as you pour out your words before Y-H-W-H.
That is why this prayer is called the *'amidah*,
 because in it you stand directly before your Master.
As we sanctify ourselves from below in this manner,
 we awaken its likeness from above.
 When we reach such an *'amidah*,
Y-H-W-H too stands directly before us, as it were.
Just as we, in standing before God,
 attach our thoughts to the central point of divinity,
 the Root of all,
 the innermost point that is the Source of all life,
So too does the blessed Holy One become concentrated
 and stand at the point of thinking of those
 who do [or "make"] God's will.
It was for their sake that He created all the worlds!
They are at the very core of God's thought,
 the foundation of all the world.[69]

Thoughts That Lead Astray

Even the distracting thoughts
        that confound you during prayer
        may be a good sign.

In a palace surrounded by many walls
        there lives a king.
At each entrance there is a guard posted,
        to keep people from approaching.
If the petitioner who comes to see the king
        is a person of no importance,
        the guards will not bother with him.
They will allow him to enter the palace undisturbed.
In any case they know
        that the king will pay him no attention.
But how different it is
        when a respected noble of the kingdom
        tries to come before the king,
        one with a request that could endanger
        the position of the guards themselves.
Then they try to put him off
        in whatever way they can,
        telling him to leave and come back some other time.
How they try to keep him from the king—
        for surely his words would be accepted
        by their master!

All this is said of prayer.
When you realize that
        you are being kept away from the King,

gather up all your strength
and cry out in anguish:
"Father, save me!"
God longs to hear His people's prayer—
one cry can open all the gates.[70]

This parable is told of prayer:

Once there was a road
    that was known to be very dangerous,
    for it passed through a forest that was filled
    with highwaymen and robbers.
These thieves would lie in wait
    for a traveler to come through the forest.
As he passed near them,
    they would pour out of their hideouts
    and fly at the throat of their victim,
    to rob for profit or simply to destroy.
Those who traveled this road were known
    to pass quickly through the forest,
    hoping to give the thieves
    no chance to fall upon them.

It happened that two men
    came to travel the way together.
One of them was very drunk, while the other was sober.
As they walked through the forest,
    the sober man pressed forward quickly
    until he had passed through the wood unharmed.
His drunken friend, however, lumbered slowly along,
    step after heavy step.
The murderers attacked him,
    beating him and covering his body
    with wounds and bruises.
But because of his drunkenness,
    he felt nothing at all.

At the far edge of the forest the two men met.
The sober man was shocked at his friend's condition
    and asked him how he had managed
    to survive the attack.
The drunk was no less shocked

at his companion's questions,
    for he believed nothing had happened to him at all.
Finally his friend brought him a looking-glass
    and showed him how battered and bruised he was
    and the bloodstains that covered his clothes.
All this baffled the drunk;
He remembered nothing at all.[71]

When a distracting thought comes to you in prayer,
    hold fast to God and break through
    to redeem the sacred spark
    that dwells within that thought.

The son of a rich man was once taken captive
    and held for ransom.
The father did nothing for his son,
    but merely sat at home, counting out his fortune.
Suddenly he saw his son before him;
The boy cried out:
"Father! What are you doing?
You have all this money—
    stop counting and redeem your son!"[72]

"If I am not for myself, who is for me?
If I am only for myself, what am I?"

A person at prayer should go beyond his own self,
        no longer feeling any attachment
        to the material world.
As long as "I am for myself,"
I cannot go beyond distraction.
Only when I no longer know my own existence
        will I be freed from all such thoughts.
When I have reached that rung of prayer
        "who is for me?"—
        if I am no longer aware of my own self,
        what distracting thought can disturb me?

"If I am only for myself"—
        if I do think of myself
        as existing in this world,
        then I am indeed nothing.
In that case, "what am I?"—
        what am I worth and of what value is my service?
Distracting thoughts will so confound me
        that I will be as nothing,
        unable to stand before Him.

And what is our existence but the service of God?[73]

"No one shall go up with you;
No one shall be seen upon that mountain."

As you stand before God in prayer,
        you should feel that you stand alone—
        in all the world only you and God exist.
Then there can be no distractions;
Nothing can disturb such prayer.[74]

Do not laugh at one who moves his body,
    even violently, during prayer.
A person drowning in a river
    makes all kinds of motions
    to try to save himself.
This is not a time for others to laugh.[75]

Prayer is never repeated:
    the quality of each day's prayer
    is unlike that of any other.
This is the inner meaning of the Mishnah's words:
    "One whose prayer is rigid
    prays without supplication."
This can be seen even in the thoughts
    that distract us from true prayer;
They too are different every day.
Each day and its prayer,
    each day and its distractions—
    until Messiah comes.[76]

The Way
of the
Simple

The tale is told of a king who one day discovered
  that the great seal of his kingdom was missing.
You cannot imagine
  how terrible was this loss for him,
  for whoever found the seal could issue decrees
  in the king's own name.
And even if no one ever did find it,
  what a disgrace
  that the king's great seal should be
  lying in the dust!
The king was saddened by his loss,
  and his sorrow was felt
  by all the royal household.
All joined in the search—
  but because they sought so carefully
  and longed so greatly to find the seal,
  they passed it by.
Then a poor farmer happened along and,
  simply glancing about,
  he came upon the seal.
Though he knew nothing of the importance of his find,
  this simple farmer brought the king great joy.
The farmer also rejoiced,
  still understanding little of what he had done,
  but saying to himself:
"The king's own seal! The king's own seal!"

  The parable is not explained.[77]

Through everything you see,
  become aware of the divine.
If you encounter love, remember the love of God.
If you experience fear, think of the fear of God.
And even in the bathroom, you should think—
  "Here I am separating bad from good,
   and the good will remain for God's service!"[78]

One who reads the words of prayer with great devotion
      may come to see the lights within the letters,
      even though one does not understand
      the meaning of the words one speaks.
Such prayer has great power;
Mistakes in reading are of no importance.

A father has a young child whom he greatly loves.
Even though the child has hardly learned to speak,
      his father takes pleasure
      in listening to the child's words.[79]

A parable is told of a person who wants to eat
    and who feels a great hunger
    for a certain food.
He then sees the very food he wants
    in a place high above him,
    beyond his reach.
In his hunger he begins to imagine
    that he is eating the food
    that he desires.
But what has he gained by such imaginings?
He is only more hungry than before.

The same is true of those who try to reach
    for the highest esoteric meaning of each prayer.
They are far from such things;
    their minds simply cannot reach
    the heights for which they strive.

Better not to reach for things beyond your grasp.[80]

The mystics have discovered many levels of meaning
    in each word of prayer.
No one person can know them all.
One who tries to meditate
    on the hidden meanings of prayer
    can only reach those secrets that can be known.

But if in prayer you join
    your whole self to every word,
    all the secret meanings
    enter the word of their own accord.
Every letter becomes a complete world.
What a great thing you do!
Worlds above are awakened by your prayer.
Thus should your prayer be fire—
    for every letter awakens worlds above.[81]

To those who move their bodies violently in prayer,
    it was told:

A candle wick may be made of cotton or of flax.
With one sort of wick
    the candle makes a great deal of noise
    as it burns,
    while the other sort of candle burns in silence.
Does the silent candle give less light?

The slightest movement of your little toe,
    if it is done in truth,
    may be sufficient.[82]

Sometimes while at prayer you may feel
    that you cannot enter
    the upper world at all.
Your mind remains below and you think:
    "The whole earth is full of His glory."
But really you are nearer to God than you know.
At such times you are like a child
    who has just begun to understand
    how close to God he is.
Even though your mind cannot yet transcend this world,
    God is with you in your prayer.[83]

How does so lowly a creature as man
 dare to come before God
 three times each day
 to seek fulfillment of his needs?

There was a king who had a garden
 in which he took great pride.
He hired a certain man to care for it:
 to plant, to trim, to cultivate the earth.
Now that gardener needed sustenance for himself
 and various supplies to tend the royal garden.
Should he be ashamed to come before the king
 each day and seek that which he needs?
It is for the king himself that he is working!

But such is not the case for a lazy worker,
 one who does nothing for the garden,
 but only takes what is given him
 to satisfy his gluttonous desires.
How can he dare to come again before the king and say:
 "Give me what I want"?[84]

We like to think that the songs and praise
　　we offer to the blessed Creator
　　magnify God and make Him even greater,
　　as they would an earthly king.

But this is not the case.
The Midrash says that we embellish
　　the praises of a king of flesh and blood
　　beyond what he deserves,
　　but the blessed Holy One is extolled
　　and yet remains infinitely more.
Regarding this the Talmud teaches: the best thing of all is silence.

God is like a priceless pearl:
　　anyone who begins to speak its praise diminishes it.
All the prayers we offer are a lessening of God indeed.
We try to squeeze the indescribably great
　　divine illumination and life force
　　into letters.
In the words of the *Tikkuney Zohar*: "No thought can grasp
　　　　You at all."
We have spoken of this struggle many times.
Yet even so our efforts are quite dear to God and much beloved.
A parable: It sometimes happens that when a father and child
　　　　are playing,
　　the child grabs hold of
　　the father's beard, hair, or some other part of his head.
The child pulls it down to his little face in order to play with it.
　　This gives the father great pleasure,
　　enjoying it even though
　　it might seem annoying and an affront to his honor.
Were anyone else to do this, it would hurt him.
But since the parent loves his child,
　　and sees that the child loves him very much
　　and longs for him as well,
　　it is clear that the child has done this out of love.

The lesson is clear: Even though our words and letters
    lessen the divine brilliance,
    God cherishes
    them as an expression of our love.[85]

A parable of prayer:

A father and his son, traveling together in a wagon,
    came to the edge of a forest.
Some bushes, thick with berries,
    caught the child's eye.
"Father," he asked, "may we stop a while
    so that I can pick some berries?"
The father was anxious to complete his journey,
    but he did not have it in his heart
    to refuse the boy's request.
The wagon was called to a halt,
    and the son alighted to pick the berries.

After a while,
    the father wanted to continue on his way.
But his son had become so engrossed in berry-picking
    that he could not bring himself
    to leave the forest.
"Son!" cried the father, "we cannot stay here all day!
We must continue our journey!"

Even his father's pleas were not enough
    to lure the boy away.
What could the father do?
Surely he loved his son no less
    for acting so childishly.
He would not think of leaving him behind—
    but he really did have to get going
    on his journey.

Finally he called out:
"You may pick your berries for a while longer,
     but be sure that you are still able to find me,
     for I shall start moving slowly along the road.
As you work, call out 'Father! Father!'
     every few minutes, and I shall answer you.
As long as you can hear my voice,
     know that I am still nearby.
But as soon as you can no longer hear my answer,
     know that you are lost,
          and run with all your strength to find me!"[86]

After
the Hour
of
Prayer

A person at prayer is like a bed of coals,
As long as a single spark remains,
       a great fire can again be kindled.
But without that spark there can be no fire.

Always remain attached to God,
       even in those times
       when you feel unable to ascend to God.
You must preserve that single spark—
       lest the fire of your soul be extinguished.[87]

Take special care of what you do in the moments
    immediately after prayer.
The spirit of your worship may remain with you
    and affect your thoughts and deeds.
One who prayed with great fear of heaven
    may see awe turn to anger.
One whose prayer was an outpouring of love
    may be overwhelmed by unwanted passion.
In order to avoid such pitfalls,
    it is best after prayer
    to begin at once your work or study.

These words require careful thought,
    but their implications are best
    not committed to writing.[88]

The hour of formal prayer is not the only time
    when you may seek to bind yourself to God.
In doing so outside the hour of prayer,
    however,
    take special care
    that no one else be near you
    as you ascend to the higher worlds.
Even the chirping of birds could disturb you;
Even the unspoken thought of another person
    could bring you back to earth.

When you seek to be alone with God,
    have at least one companion with you.
Alone one is in danger.
When two are in the same room,
    each of them may turn to God separately.
When you are more experienced,
    you may sometimes meditate alone in a room—
    But surely someone else should be
    in the same house with you.[89]

There are times when you are not at prayer,
    but nevertheless you can feel close to God.
Your mind can ascend even above the heavens.

And there are also times,
    in the very midst of prayer,
        when you find yourself unable to ascend.
At such times stand where you are
    and serve with love.[90]

A
Final
Parable

 This parable is told:

There was once a musician,
    well-known for the great beauty
    of his music, who came to play before the king.
One particular melody was so loved by the king
    that he ordered the musician
    to play it for him several times each day.
And so it was.
After a time, however,
    the musician began to weary of the tune;
    no longer could he play it with the same passion
    and excitement as before.

The king, to rekindle his musician's love
    for this favorite tune,
    ordered that a person be brought in from the market,
    one who had never heard the tune before.
Seeing someone who had never heard him play,
    the musician's vigor was renewed,
    and he played the tune in all its beauty,
Thus the king ordered a new person brought each day.

After some time, the king sought other counsel,
    for to find a new audience each day
    was not an easy matter.
It was decided that the musician should be blinded,
    so that he never see a human form again.
Now the blind musician sat before the king,
    and whenever the king sought
    to hear his favorite tune
    he would simply say:
    "Here comes someone new,
    one who has never heard you play before!"
And the musician would play his tune
    with the greatest joy.

The parable is not explained.[91]

NOTES

1 *Likkutim Yekarim*, no. 22, fol. 4b.

2 *Maggid Devarav le-Ya'akov*, no. 39, pp. 59–60. "Who is like Your Israel," from 2 Samuel 7:23, is invoked in the Shabbat afternoon liturgy.

3 *Me'or 'Eynayim*, vol. 1, *va-ethanan*, pp. 325 and 319. The source for the opening quotation is Isaiah 40:2, and "Let them pray to You through their land" is 1 Kings 8:48.

4 *Or ha-Me'ir*, vol. 2, *derush le-shabbat teshuvah*, p. 273. This translation is a free rendition hoping to recapture the spirit of this dialogue. For a more literal translation and discussion of the passage, see Gershom Scholem, *The Messianic Idea in Judaism and Other Essays on Jewish Spirituality* (New York: Schocken Books, 1971), p. 242.

5 *Toledot Ya'akov Yosef*, vol. 3, *'ekev*, p. 1183.

6 *Tif'eret 'Uzi'el, pesah*, p. 134.

7 *Kedushat Levi*, vol. 2, *likkutim*, p. 455. Biblical quotation is from Psalm 106:2.

8 *Or ha-Hokhmah*, vol. 2, *be-ha'alotekha*, pp. 31–32.

9 *'Avodat Yisra'el, likkutim*, pp. 220–221. The text begins with a quotation from *Shulhan 'Arukh, orah hayyim* 55:13. The biblical quotation is from 1 Kings 8:32.

10 *Kedushat Levi*, vol. 1, *va-yelekh*, pp. 431–432; based on the translation in Arthur Green et al., *Speaking Torah: Spiritual Teachings from around the Maggid's Table* (Woodstock, VT: Jewish Lights, 2013), vol. 2, p. 138. For "going down" before the ark, think of ancient amphitheater-like synagogues. The reference is to b. Shabbat 24b. For "passing before" the ark, see b. Berakhot 34a. The reference to Moses indicates that according to the *Zohar* (*Zohar* 3:275b) he was "higher" than *shekhinah*, the rung of divine word. In Hebrew *tevah* means both "ark" and "word."

11 *Degel Mahaneh Efrayim*, *'ekev*, p. 507. The two quotations are from the daily liturgy and from Psalm 71:9.

12 *Likkutim Yekarim*, no. 136, fol. 45a–b; *Keter Shem Tov*, no. 212, pp. 120–121.

13 *Tsava'at ha-Rivash*, no. 16, p. 7. "The Master" here is the Ba'al Shem Tov. Kabbalists placed great emphasis upon the sacred quality of the hours of

dawn and dusk as proper times for prayer. Cf. *Magen Avraham* to *Shul-han 'Arukh, orah hayyim* 1:1. According to the *Zohar* (1:178a), the central *'amidah* prayer, which on weekdays contains a series of petitions, should be recited immediately *after* the rising of the sun, as the moments preceding sunrise are too intimate to be interrupted by mere petition.

14 *Hit'orerut ha-Tefillah*, fol. 3a–b. The quotation is from Ecclesiastes 5:1.

15 *Tsava'at ha-Rivash*, no. 107, p. 49.

16 *Tsava'at ha-Rivash*, no. 42, p. 16; *Likkutim Yekarim*, no. 2, fol. 1a. The present translation is a conflation of several versions.

17 *Toledot Ya'akov Yosef*, vol. 2, *tazri'a*, pp. 584–585.

18 *Tsava'at ha-Rivash*, no. 32, p. 13. There are times, however, when the masters recommend that the worshiper rush quickly through the words of prayer—perhaps so that distractions will have no chance to grab hold. Cf. pp. 106–107 and note 71 below.

19 *Me'or 'Eynayim, likkutim*, p. 443. The opening quotation is from m. Avot 4:16. "One guard higher than the next" is from Ecclesiastes 5:7.

20 *Hit'orerut ha-Tefillah*, fol. 7b.

21 *Pitgamin Kaddishin*, fol. 7a. While the importance of music in Hasidism is well-known and the wordless *niggun* became a characteristic Hasidic form of contemplation, the masters opposed the conversion of the liturgy into a platform for the "artistic" cantor.

22 This is a series of interpretations of Genesis 6:14, based on the dual meaning of the word *tevah*, the biblical term for "ark," which can also mean "word" in Rabbinic Hebrew. *Or ha-Me'ir, be-shalah*, vol. 1, p. 128; *Toledot Yitshak*, p. 7; *Tsava'at ha-Rivash*, no. 75, pp. 31–32. Another version in *Degel Mahaneh Efrayim, noah*, pp. 18–19.

23 *Shemu'ah Tovah*, fol. 73b. The phrase "the great, the powerful, and the awesome" is found in the first blessing of the daily *'amidah* prayer, derived in turn from Deuteronomy 10:17. According to the Kabbalists, each of these adjectives represents a particular aspect of the Divine Self: "the great" is divine love (*hesed*), "the powerful" is divine judgment (*din*), and "the awesome" is divine majesty (*tif'eret*), which mediates between the two others.

24 *Tsava'at ha-Rivash*, no. 108, p. 50.

25 *Darkhey Tsedek*, no. 39, fol. 6b. The creation of the universe by means of the letters of the Hebrew alphabet is a well-known motif in Jewish literature.

26 *Keter Shem Tov*, no. 387b, pp. 235–236.

27 *Likkutim Yekarim*, no. 2, fol. 1a; *Tsava'at ha-Rivash*, no. 34, p. 14.

28 *Keter Shem Tov*, no. 284b, p. 164, quoting Psalm 97:11.

29 *Or ha-Emet*, fol. 36b. This is the heart of mystical union as portrayed in Hasidism: the human soul is itself a part of God, cut off from its sources by the veil (or illusion, in some schools) of separate existence. In prayer and contemplation, that of God that dwells within the soul, "your" God in this passage, is united with God beyond. The passage from Deuteronomy 10:12 is taken as though it read "with the Lord—*your* God."

30 *Likkutim Yekarim*, no. 136, fol. 45b, based on the rereading of Psalm 150:6 in *Bereshit Rabbah* 14:9.

31 *Or Torah, ki tissa*, no. 105, pp. 145–147. Quotation from *Zohar* 1:5a.

32 *Maggid Devarav le-Ya'akov*, no. 13, pp. 26–27.

33 *Or ha-Me'ir*, vol. 1, *shir ha-shirim*, p. 263.

34 *Me'or 'Eynayim*, vol. 1, *ki tissa*, p. 200. For "Whoever sets a fixed place for his prayer, the God of Abraham helps him," see b. Berakhot 6b. This text offers a particularly vivid description of prayer, filled with words that swirl about one, without the ability to break through the swirls in a clear arrow-like trajectory.

35 *Torey Zahav, noah*, p. 16. See note 22, above.

36 *Or ha-Emet*, fol. 2b.

37 *Maggid Devarav le-Ya'akov*, no. 110, p. 186. The term "World of Thought" is a common Hasidic designation for the deepest and most hidden of the divine manifestations (*sefirot*). The World of Thought comes to be revealed in the World of Speech, the lowest of the ten manifestations, also called *shekhinah* (Presence), in a way parallel to the revelation of a person's deepest thoughts in spoken words. The upper sefirotic realm, that of *hokhmah* or *binah* (Thought), is one of complete unity, where distinctions of individual identity and moral judgment have not yet come to be.

38 *Shemu'ah Tovah*, fol. 79b–80a.

39 *Maggid Devarav le-Ya'akov*, no. 110, p. 186. "Endless" here is used to translate *Eyn Sof*, the Kabbalistic term for the hidden Godhead. It literally means "without end."

40 *'Avodat Yisra'el, metsora'*, p. 117. The author explains that one's ability to go on with reciting the liturgy at such moments surely must be a divine gift.

41 *Shemu'ah Tovah*, fol. 80a. The comment is on the thrice-daily recitation of Psalm 51:17 as an introduction to the *'amidah* prayer. The Hebrew word *safah* may mean either "lip" or "riverbank." See also the following text.

42 *Maggid Devarav le-Ya'akov*, no. 2, p. 13.

43 *Tsava'at ha-Rivash*, no. 36, p. 14; *Keter Shem Tov*, no. 220c–d, pp. 126–127. The latter source describes such a devotee as one "drunk" with prayer. The *Tsava'at ha-Rivash* version, used in this translation, deletes the word *shikor*.

Hasidim, who were accused by their enemies of excessive drinking, may have chosen to censor such a positive reference to spiritual inebriation in their early literature.

44 *Maggid Devarav le-Ya'akov*, no. 106, p. 184. The ram's horn (shofar) is used in Jewish liturgy, especially on the New Year, recalling the ram who replaced Isaac on the altar. See also note 37 for more about the World of Speech and the World of Thought.

45 *Tsava'at ha-Rivash*, no. 137, p. 66. "From afar God appears to me" is from Jeremiah 31:3. The respective values placed on the two prayer states should not be oversimplified: while *gadlut* is generally taken to be the ideal state for worship, statements in praise of the simple devotion of *katnut* are by no means lacking in Hasidic literature. Cf. pp. 121 and 132.

46 *Likkutim Yekarim*, no. 45, fol. 11a.

47 *Me'or 'Eynayim*, vol. 2, *likkutim*, p. 509 (abbreviated). The first biblical quotation is Genesis 27:22. Note also: "Jacob said I am too small for all the grace you have done for your servant" (Genesis 32:11). "God despises all those of haughty heart" is from Proverbs 16:5.

48 *Me'or 'Eynayim*, vol. 2, *likkutim*, pp. 443–444. The biblical quotation is Song of Songs 8:7, but the writer is reading the Hebrew *boz yavuzu* not as the usual "they would surely mock him," but as in the sense of "despoiling," carting away a large load of blessings.

49 *Me'or 'Eynayim*, vol. 1, *ha'azinu*, pp. 370–371. "I will dwell among them" is from Exodus 25:8. "The throne (*kisse*) is not whole" is from *Midrash Tanhuma, tetse*, no. 11. Exodus 17:16, occurring in the context of Israel's battle with Amalek, is written *ki yad 'al kes Yah*; the word "throne" lacks its final aleph. "The whole earth be filled with His glory" is from Isaiah 6:3. "As I call upon the name Y-H-W-H, give greatness to our God" is from Deuteronomy 32:3. For "Israel gives strength to God," see Psalm 68:35.

50 *Peri ha-Arets, va-yeshev*, pp. 143–146. For "removed the soiled garments," see Zechariah 3:4. The verse "Come in, you and all your household, to the word" (Genesis 7:1), from the Noah story, takes the Hebrew word *tevah* from the verse not as "ark" but in its other meaning, "word." "Spread your wing over your maidservant" is from Ruth 3:9. "Those who have tasted of her have attained life" is a phrase from the *Musaf* (additional) service recited on the Sabbath.

51 *Heikhal ha-Berakhah*, vol. 4, fol. 82a. "Prayer" as a name for *shekhinah* is found in earlier mystical literature. Hanina ben Dosa was a great wonder-worker and master of prayer in the first century.

52 *Sefer Ba'al Shem Tov*, vol. 1, *noah—'amud ha-tefillah*, fn. 118, pp. 176–177. Quoted in the name of Aaron of Kaidanov, presumably by oral tradition.

53 *Toledot Ya'akov Yosef,* vol. 3, *va-ethanan,* p. 1164. A comment on Psalm 102:1. It is made obvious in the context that neither the king nor his beloved servant will want for lack of treasures—but such treasures are not a worthy object of prayer.

54 *'Avodat Yisra'el, likkutim,* pp. 201–202. Biblical quotations are from Deuteronomy 24:11–12, Psalm 51:19, and Exodus 22:26. The author, quoting from memory, conflated the Deuteronomy and Exodus verses.

55 *Degel Mahaneh Efrayim, ki tetse,* pp. 544–545. The passage is a comment on the saying of Antigonus of Sokho in Avot 1:3. On the two versions in that source, cf. the commentary of Rabbenu Yonah Gerondi ad loc.

56 *Toledot Ya'akov Yosef,* vol. 1, *va-era,* pp. 275–276. The reference is to the prayer *ahavat 'olam* (Eternal Love), which immediately precedes the recitation of the *shema',* the proclamation of God's unity that is the center of Jewish worship.

57 *Tsava'at ha-Rivash,* no. 85, pp. 36–37.

58 *Orah le-Hayyim,* p. 386. Hasidic teachings claim that everything, including suffering and evil, comes from God. While on one level this recognition is the basis for even the beginning of a prayer life, final acceptance of it can be seen only as prayer's most ultimate goal.

59 *Hit'orerut ha-Tefillah,* fol. 4a. Based on a Midrashic source; cf. Jellinek's *Bet ha-Midrash* 1:63 (*Midrash 'Aseret ha-Dibrot*). The biblical text is Lamentations 2:19.

60 *Ketonet Passim, balak,* p. 326. Based on an explanation of *Tur, orah hayyim* 5, which discusses the difference in meaning between the ineffable name Y-H-W-H and the reading *Adonai,* as the name is pronounced in the liturgy.

61 *Tsava'at ha-Rivash,* no. 68, p. 28. The sexual metaphor is often applied to prayer in early Hasidic literature. A passage in *Toledot Ya'akov Yosef,* in which the Ba'al Shem Tov is said to have called the daily *'amidah* "the true embrace and coupling" is a paraphrase of such earlier sources as *Zohar* 2:128b, but with an important difference. To the earlier mystics, the coupling was envisioned as taking place *within* God; in the Hasidic reading, it is God and the worshiper who are locked in the embrace of intimacy.

62 *Tsava'at ha-Rivash,* no. 137, p. 66.

63 *Keter Shem Tov,* no. 192, p. 106. The term *devekut* is central to Hasidic thought, particularly in the school of Dov Baer of Mezritsh, and is given many definitions in Hasidic literature. For a discussion of this term and its implications, see Scholem, "*Devekuth* or Communion with God," in *The Messianic Idea in Judaism,* pp. 203–227.

64 *Or ha-Emet,* fol. 2b. The quotation is from the literature of Merkavah mysticism.

65 *Likkutim Yekarim*, no. 192, fol. 58a–58b.

66 *Tsava'at ha-Rivash*, no. 105, p. 45; *Keter Shem Tov*, no. 233b, pp. 131–132. The forces of evil are commonly described in Kabbalistic sources as *kelipot* (shells) that seek to hide the light of divinity from the world.

67 *Tsava'at ha-Rivash*, no. 33, p. 14. The quotation is from Psalm 35:10.

68 *Ketonet Passim*, *balak*, p. 326. The right hand of God is traditionally associated with divine love, while the left signifies divine might and rigor.

69 *Shemen ha-Tov*, *nitsavim*, fol. 13a–b (based on *Kedushat Levi*, vol. 1, *be-shalah*, pp. 193–194; in Green et al., *Speaking Torah*, vol. 2, pp. 132–133). The source for "standing" meaning "prayer" is b. Berakhot 6b. The biblical quotation is from Psalm 106:30.

70 *Sefat Emet* (by Meshulam Feibush of Brezhan), *va-yera*, as cited in *Sefer Ba'al Shem Tov*, vol. 1, *noah—'amud ha-tefillah*, no. 105, pp. 155–156.

71 *Divrey Moshe*, fol. 35a. The parable, attributed by the Ba'al Shem Tov to his brother-in-law Rabbi Gershon Kitover, seems to recommend rapid prayer, so that distractions will not have a chance to enter the worshiper's mind. A shorter version of the same parable is used to prove a rather different point in *Toledot Ya'akov Yosef*, vol. 3, *ki tavo*, p. 1327.

72 *Likkutim Yekarim*, no. 184, fol. 57b.

73 *Likkutim Yekarim*, no. 41, fol. 6b–7a. The passage is a comment on Hillel's dictum in m. Avot 1:14, offering a strikingly radical rereading of the original passage.

74 *Ben Porat Yosef*, *likkutim*, vol. 2, p. 492. A comment on Exodus 34:3.

75 *Likkutim Yekarim*, no. 167, fol. 55a–b; *Keter Shem Tov*, no. 115, pp. 122–123.

76 *Toledot Ya'akov Yosef*, vol. 1, *va-yakhel*, p. 479. The quotation is from m. Berakhot 4:4, here interpreted to mean that one should make the fixed prayer sufficiently flexible to allow for the special qualities of each day.

77 *Likkutim Yekarim*, no. 45, fol. 8a. Truth, according to the rabbis, is God's royal seal.

78 *Tsava'at ha-Rivash*, no. 22, p. 9. The Krakow and some other later editions read *bet ha-kenesset* (synagogue) instead of *bet ha-kisse* (bathroom), perhaps a printer's error based on a confusion of abbreviations!

79 See *Likkutim Yekarim*, no. 3, fol. 1a–b.

80 *Or ha-Me'ir*, vol. 1, *va-yera*, p. 31. On early Hasidic attitudes toward esoteric prayer, see Joseph Weiss, "The Kavvanoth of Prayer in Early Hasidism," *Studies in East European Jewish Mysticism and Hasidism*, ed. David Goldstein (Oxford: Littman Library of Jewish Civilization, 1997), pp. 99–105, where the present text is discussed; and Menachem Kallus, "The

Relation of the Baal Shem Tov to the Practice of Lurianic *Kavvanot* in Light of His Comments on the Siddur Rashkov," *Kabbalah* 2 (1997): 151–167.

81 *Tsava'at ha-Rivash*, no. 118, pp. 54–55; *Likkutim Yekarim*, no. 227, fol. 67a–67b. This text too is discussed in Weiss's article mentioned in the preceding note.

82 *Botsina de-Nehora*, vol. 2, p. 18.

83 *Tsava'at ha-Rivash*, no. 67, p. 18. Cf. Isaiah 6:3.

84 *Dibrat Shlomo, naso*, pp. 302–303.

85 *Dibrat Shlomo, terumah*, pp. 182–183. The text from the Midrash is *Tanhuma, shemot*, no. 2. For "anyone who begins to speak its praise diminishes it," see y. Berakhot 9:1.

86 *Divrey Shmuel*, p. 124.

87 *Likkutim Yekarim*, no. 171, fol. 55b–56a; *Keter Shem Tov*, no. 217b, p. 124.

88 *Degel Mahaneh Efrayim, ki tissa*, p. 286.

89 *Keter Shem Tov*, no. 216b, p. 123; *Likkutim Yekarim*, no. 175, fol. 56a–b; ibid, no. 13, fol. 3a; *Tsava'at ha-Rivash*, no. 63, p. 26. Here the sources reflect two seemingly contradictory counsels. Could the latter be a warning against the dangers of the former?

90 *Tsava'at ha-Rivash*, no. 136, p. 65.

91 *Or ha-Me'ir*, vol. 2, *kohelet*, p. 314. The parable is quoted in the name of the Ba'al Shem Tov. The author of *Or ha-Me'ir* offers the suggestion that man must be blind to this world in order to see the other—an explanation that seems to escape rather than confront the frightening reality of this parable.

SUGGESTIONS FOR FURTHER READING

Many of the texts included in this volume are attributed to the Ba'al Shem Tov. Culled from many sources, these were compiled in a special section of *Sefer Ba'al Shem Tov*, an exhaustive collection of teachings in his name, first published in Lodz, 1938. That entire section, titled *'Amud ha-Tefillah*, has now been translated and extensively annotated by Menachem Kallus as *The Pillar of Prayer* (Louisville: Fons Vitae, 2011).

Texts from the *Me'or 'Eynayim*, added in this edition, will appear in Arthur Green's complete translation of that work, to be published in the Yale Judaica Series in 2018. Some of those and other early Hasidic prayer texts also appear in *Speaking Torah: Teachings from around the Maggid's Table*, by Arthur Green with Ebn Leader, Ariel Evan Mayse, and Or N. Rose (Woodstock, VT: Jewish Lights, 2013). Norman Lamm's anthology *The Religious Thought of Hasidism: Text and Commentary*, with Alan Brill and Shalom Carmy (Hoboken: Yeshiva University Press, 1999), also contains an important section on prayer, including materials from later Hasidic generations.

Scholarly treatments of Hasidic prayer are to be found in Rivka Schatz Uffenheimer's *Hasidism as Mysticism: Quietistic Elements in Eighteenth-Century Hasidic Thought*, translated by Jonathan Chipman (Princeton: Princeton University Press, 1993), and Louis Jacobs's *Hasidic Prayer* (London: Littman Library, 1972).

A modern treatment of Jewish prayer deeply influenced by the Hasidic sources is Abraham Joshua Heschel's *Man's Quest for God: Studies in Prayer and Symbolism* (New York: Scribner, 1954; reprint, 1982). Several works by Zalman Schachter-Shalomi, including *Davening: A Guide to Meaningful Jewish Prayer*, with Joel Segal (Woodstock, VT: Jewish Lights, 2012), present prayer in a neo-Hasidic spirit, partially shaped by the sources represented here. His writings and those of Lawrence Kushner and Nehemia Polen (*Filling Words with Light: Hasidic and Mystical Reflections on Jewish Prayer* [Woodstock, VT: Jewish Lights, 2004]) and Jonathan Slater (*A Partner in Holiness: Deepening Mindfulness, Practicing Compassion and Enriching Our Lives through the Wisdom of R. Levi Yitzhak of Berdichev's* Kedushat Levi [Woodstock, VT: Jewish Lights, 2014]) present Hasidic sources in a contemporary meditative context.

EDITIONS OF HASIDIC WORKS CITED

'Avodat Yisra'el. Jerusalem, 1996.

Ben Porat Yosef. Jerusalem, 2011. 2 vols.

Botsina de-Nehora. Jerusalem, 2007. 2 vols.

Darkhey Tsedek. Lvov, 1877.

Degel Mahaneh Efrayim. Jerusalem, 2013.

Dibrat Shlomo. Jerusalem, 2011.

Divrey Moshe. Israel, 1965.

Divrey Shmuel. Jerusalem, 1954.

Heikhal ha-Berakhah. Lvov, 1864.

Hit'orerut ha-Tefillah. Piotrkow, 1911.

Kedushat Levi ha-Shalem. Jerusalem, 2007. 2 vols.

Keter Shem Tov ha-Shalem. Brooklyn, 2004.

Ketonet Passim. Jerusalem, 2011.

Likkutim Yekarim. Jerusalem, 1974.

Maggid Devarav le-Ya'akov, ed. Rivka Schatz Uffenheimer. Jerusalem, 1976.

Me'or 'Eynayim. Jerusalem, 2012. 2 vols.

Or ha-Emet. Brooklyn, 1960.

Or ha-Hokhmah. Jerusalem, 1970. 2 vols.

Or ha-Me'ir. Jerusalem, 2000. 2 vols.

Or Torah ha-Shalem. Brooklyn, 2011.

Orah le-Hayyim. Jerusalem, 1960.

Peri ha-Arets. Beitar Illit, 2014. 2 vols.

Pitgamin Kaddishin. Warsaw, 1886.

Sefer Ba'al Shem Tov 'al ha-Torah. Jerusalem, 2007. 2 vols.

Shemen ha-Tov. Piotrkov, 1905.

Shemu'ah Tovah. Warsaw, 1938.

Tif'eret 'Uzi'el. Tel Aviv, 1962.

Toledot Ya'akov Yosef. Jerusalem, 2011. 3 vols.

Toledot Yitshak. Ashdod, 1968.

Torey Zahav. Jerusalem, 2013.

Tsava'at ha-Rivash. Brooklyn, 1998.

ABOUT THE AUTHORS

ARTHUR GREEN, a historian of Jewish religion and a theologian, is the founding dean of the Rabbinical School of Hebrew College and now serves as its rector. He has lectured widely and taught Jewish mysticism, Hasidism, and theology to several generations of students at the University of Pennsylvania; the Reconstructionist Rabbinical College, where he served as both dean and president; Brandeis University; and Hebrew College. Green is the founder of Havurat Shalom, an egalitarian Jewish community in Somerville, Massachusetts, and remains a leading independent neo-Hasidic teacher. He is the author or editor of more than a dozen books, including *Speaking Torah: Spiritual Teachings from around the Maggid's Table* (Woodstock, VT: Jewish Lights, 2013) and *Judaism's Ten Best Ideas: A Brief Guide for Seekers* (Woodstock, VT: Jewish Lights, 2014). His *Radical Judaism: Rethinking God and Tradition* (New Haven: Yale University Press, 2010) was recently published in Hebrew (Rishon leZion: Yediot Ahronoth, 2016).

BARRY W. HOLTZ is the Theodore and Florence Baumritter Professor of Jewish Education at The Jewish Theological Seminary. From 2008 to 2013 he served as dean of the seminary's William Davidson Graduate School of Jewish Education. His books include *Back to the Sources: Reading the Classic Jewish Texts* (New York: Simon and Schuster, 2006), *Finding Our Way: Jewish Texts and the Lives We Lead Today* (New York: Schocken Books, 1990), *Textual Knowledge: Teaching the Bible in Theory and in Practice*, and most recently *Rabbi Akiva: Sage of the Talmud* (New Haven: Yale University Press, 2016).

ARIEL EVAN MAYSE joined the faculty of Stanford University in 2017 as an assistant professor in the department of religious studies. He previously served as the director of Jewish studies and visiting assistant professor of modern Jewish thought at Hebrew College in Newton, Massachusetts. He holds a PhD in Jewish studies from Harvard

University and rabbinic ordination from Beit Midrash Har'el. In addition to scholarly and popular articles on Jewish mysticism, he is coauthor of the two-volume collection *Speaking Torah: Spiritual Teachings from around the Maggid's Table* (Woodstock, VT: Jewish Lights, 2013) and editor of *From the Depth of the Well: An Anthology of Jewish Mysticism* (Mahwah, NJ: Paulist Press, 2014). Green and Mayse are coeditors of *A New Hasidism: Roots and Branches* (Philadelphia: Jewish Publication Society, 2018).

Printed in the USA
CPSIA information can be obtained
at www.ICGtesting.com
JSHW082211140824
68134JS00014B/563